Table of Contents

INTRODUCTION	2
CHAPTER 1: INTRODUCTION TO VENTURE CAPITAL	4
CHAPTER 2: THE VENTURE CAPITAL PROCESS	6
CHAPTER 3: TYPES OF VENTURE CAPITAL FIRMS	9
CHAPTER 4: UNDERSTANDING TERM SHEETS	12
CHAPTER 5: FUNDING ROUNDS EXPLAINED	15
CHAPTER 6: THE ROLE OF VENTURE CAPITALISTS	18
CHAPTER 7: RISKS AND REWARDS OF VENTURE CAPITAL	21
CHAPTER 8: EXIT STRATEGIES IN VENTURE CAPITAL	24
CHAPTER 9: CURRENT TRENDS IN VENTURE CAPITAL	27
CHAPTER 10: BUILDING RELATIONSHIPS WITH VENTURE CAPITALISTS	30
CHAPTER 11: RESOURCES FOR ENTREPRENEURS	33
CONCLUSION	36

Chapter 1: Introduction to Venture Capital

1. What is venture capital?

Venture capital is money invested in new companies that have a big chance to grow. Investors give this money in exchange for a share of the company.

2. How is venture capital different from a bank loan?

With venture capital, you don't have to pay the money back like a loan. Instead, the investors get part of the company and share in the profits if it does well.

3. Why do startups need venture capital?

Startups often need venture capital to build products, hire people, and grow quickly. They usually don't have enough money on their own or access to bank loans.

4. What types of companies look for venture capital?

Technology, healthcare, and energy startups often look for venture capital because they need a lot of money to grow and can bring big profits.

5. Who are venture capitalists?

Venture capitalists are people or groups that invest money in startups. They hope these companies will grow and make a lot of money.

6. Why do venture capitalists invest in risky companies?

Venture capitalists invest in risky companies because they hope to earn big profits if the company succeeds.

Venture Capital Basics Q&A

by

Pinnacle Press

VENTURE
CAPITAL
BASICS

Q&A

PINNACLE PRESS

Introduction

Venture Capital Basics Q&A, explains how venture capital helps startups grow by providing money, advice, and connections. It's written for entrepreneurs, business professionals, and investors who want to understand how venture capital works.

The book covers important topics like the types of venture capital firms, how funding works, and the importance of building relationships with investors. It also explains things like term sheets, funding rounds, and strategies for exiting investments. New trends like focusing on sustainability and diversity are also discussed.

Getting venture capital can be tough, but this book offers clear advice to help you make better choices, connect with investors, and succeed in your business goals. The world of venture capital is always changing, and learning about it will help you handle challenges and find new opportunities.

Welcome to the world of venture capital, where new ideas become successful businesses.

7. Is venture capital easy to get?

No, it's hard to get. Startups need to prove they have a great idea and a strong plan to grow.

8. Has venture capital changed over time?

Yes, it has grown to include more industries like tech and green energy. There are now more investors and more money being invested.

9. What's the future of venture capital?

Venture capital will likely focus more on technology and businesses that help the environment as these areas grow.

Chapter 2: The Venture Capital Process

1. What are the key stages of the venture capital process?

The venture capital process has several stages:

Finding Startups: Looking for companies to invest in.
Initial Check: Reviewing business ideas to decide if they're worth more attention.
Deep Research: Checking the company's finances, market, and team in detail.
Making the Deal: Agreeing on how much to invest and the terms of the deal.
Helping the Company: Giving advice, joining the board, and helping the company grow.
Selling Shares: Selling the shares later through an IPO or a buyout.

2. How do venture capitalists decide which companies to invest in?

Venture capitalists look at:

Market: Is there a big and growing market?
Business Idea: Can the company make money?
Team: Are the founders experienced and capable?
Product: Is it unique and better than competitors?
Proof of Success: Does the company already have customers or sales?

3. Why is due diligence important?

Due diligence is when investors check everything about the company before investing. It helps them avoid surprises by looking at finances, legal issues, and market data.

4. What factors influence the decision to invest?

Investors think about:

Risk: How risky is the business?
Returns: How much money can they make?
Trends: Is the industry growing?
Match: Does the investor's expertise fit the company?

5. How are investment terms agreed upon?

Founders and investors discuss key points like:

Valuation: How much is the company worth?
Ownership: How much of the company the investor gets.
Control: Whether the investor gets a say in decisions.

6. What types of investment deals are common?

Common investment deals include:

Equity: Buying part of the company.
Convertible Notes: Loans that turn into shares later.
SAFE: An agreement to get shares in the future.

7. What do board members do in venture-backed companies?

Board members help guide the company's plans, give advice, connect the company to resources, and make sure it's on track to succeed.

8. How do venture capitalists help after investing?

Venture capitalists support companies by:

Giving advice and mentoring.
Helping hire important staff.
Connecting the company to their network.
Raising more funds when needed.

9. What challenges do venture capitalists face?

Venture capitalists deal with:

Finding good startups in a busy market.
Balancing risks with potential rewards.
Working well with founders.
Adapting to changes in the economy.
Getting good returns when selling shares.

Chapter 3: Types of Venture Capital Firms

1. What are the different types of venture capital firms?

Venture capital firms can be divided into these types:

Early-Stage Firms: Focus on new startups in the first funding rounds (Seed or Series A).
Growth-Stage Firms: Invest in companies that are growing and need funds to expand (Series B or later).
Sector-Specific Firms: Specialize in industries like tech, healthcare, or clean energy.
Corporate Venture Capital: Funded by big companies to invest in startups related to their business.
Micro VCs: Smaller firms that focus on early-stage investments with smaller amounts of money.

2. How do corporate venture capital firms differ from traditional VC firms?

Corporate VC firms are part of big companies and invest in startups to help their business, not just to earn money. Traditional VCs mainly focus on making profits from their investments.

3. What are angel investors, and how do they fit into venture capital?

Angel investors are individuals who use their own money to invest in early-stage startups. They help startups get started before they are ready for bigger VC funding.

4. What are early-stage VC firms like?

Early-stage VC firms:

Take big risks for high rewards.

Look for new ideas and strong teams.
Invest smaller amounts of money.
Help startups grow with advice and support.

5. How do growth-stage VC firms work?

Growth-stage VC firms:

Invest in companies that are already growing.
Provide large amounts of money to help with expansion.
Look at business growth, revenues, and customer numbers.

6. What do sector-specific VC firms do?

Sector-specific VC firms focus on one industry, like tech or healthcare. They use their knowledge of the industry to choose startups and provide helpful advice.

7. What role do micro VCs play?

Micro VCs focus on smaller investments, usually for new startups. They help founders get their business started and provide hands-on support.

8. What are the pros and cons of working with different types of VC firms?

Pros:

Early-Stage Firms: Provide lots of advice and understand startup needs.
Growth-Stage Firms: Have money and resources to help scale fast.
Sector-Specific Firms: Offer industry expertise.
Corporate VCs: Provide business partnerships and market insights.
Micro VCs: Give personal attention and are flexible.

Cons:

Early-Stage Firms: May not have funds for later growth.
Growth-Stage Firms: Might expect fast results.
Sector-Specific Firms: Limited to one industry.
Corporate VCs: May focus on their own company's goals.
Micro VCs: Smaller budgets can limit growth support.

9. How can entrepreneurs choose the right VC firm?

Entrepreneurs should:

Pick a firm that shares their vision.
Look for firms with experience in their industry.
Find one that matches their funding stage and needs.
Choose a firm that offers support beyond just money.
Check the firm's reputation and connections in the market.

Chapter 4: Understanding Term Sheets

1. What is a term sheet?

A term sheet is a document that lists the main points of a deal between a startup and a venture capital firm. It is not final, but it helps both sides agree on the key terms before signing a detailed contract.

2. Why are term sheets important?

Term sheets are important because they make sure everyone agrees on the main points of the deal. This prevents confusion later and helps both sides work through the details more easily.

3. What are the key parts of a term sheet?

The key parts of a term sheet are:

Valuation: How much the company is worth before and after the investment.
Investment Amount: How much money is being invested.
Equity Stake: The share of the company the investor gets.
Type of Security: What kind of investment (like preferred stock or convertible notes).
Dividends: Rules about profit sharing.
Liquidation Preference: Who gets paid first if the company is sold.
Voting Rights: What decisions investors can vote on.
Board Seats: Agreements about who gets to be on the board of directors.
Protective Provisions: Rights investors have for important decisions.
Exit Strategy: How the investors plan to make money, like through a sale or IPO.

4. How is valuation decided in a term sheet?

Valuation is decided through talks between the founders and investors. It depends on things like how well the company is doing, the size of its market, and how similar companies are valued.

5. What is liquidation preference, and why is it important?

Liquidation preference decides who gets paid first if the company is sold or shut down. It protects investors by making sure they get their money back before others, like the founders or employees, receive anything.

6. How do dividends work in venture capital?

Dividends are payments to investors from company profits. In startups, they are often not paid out because profits are reinvested. If dividends are in the term sheet, it's clear how and when investors might get these payments.

7. What are protective provisions?

Protective provisions are rules that let investors have a say in big company decisions, like selling the company or issuing new shares. This protects their investment.

8. How can founders negotiate better term sheet terms?

Founders can:

Know the Market: Research what's standard for their industry.
Show Growth Potential: Use data to prove their company is worth the investment.
Build Trust: Have good communication with investors.
Stay Flexible: Be willing to compromise on some points to get a fair deal.

9. What mistakes should founders avoid when reviewing term sheets?

Founders should avoid:

Skipping Details: Not carefully reading the term sheet.
Ignoring Future Needs: Forgetting how terms affect future funding rounds.
Not Using a Lawyer: Skipping legal advice.
Rushing: Agreeing too quickly without fully understanding the terms.

10. What happens after the term sheet is signed?

After signing the term sheet, due diligence happens. This means both sides check all the details about the company. Then, final legal documents are written and signed to complete the investment.

Chapter 5: Funding Rounds Explained

1. What are funding rounds?

Funding rounds are stages where startups raise money to grow their business. Each round is tied to specific goals, like developing a product, expanding operations, or preparing for an exit.

2. What are the main types of funding rounds?

The main types are:

Seed Round: Early money to test an idea or build a prototype.
Series A: Funding to grow the business and gain market traction.
Series B: Money for expanding operations and reaching more customers.
Series C and Beyond: Larger investments for scaling, entering new markets, or preparing for an IPO or sale.

3. How do startups decide when to raise funds?

Startups raise funds when they:

Reach key milestones (like launching a product).
Need cash to take advantage of market opportunities.
Are running low on money but still have growth potential.
Have clear goals that require extra funding, like entering new markets.

4. What is a convertible note, and when is it used?

A convertible note is a loan that turns into equity during a future funding round. It's often used in early funding rounds because it doesn't require setting a company valuation right away.

5. What are the pros and cons of seed funding?

Pros:

Provides money to build and test a business idea.
Attracts credibility from investors.
May include mentorship and connections.

Cons:

Founders give up some ownership early.
Investors may pressure founders to meet milestones quickly.
Goals may not always align between founders and investors.

6. How does Series A funding differ from seed funding?

Seed funding is for developing an idea or prototype. Series A funding is for scaling the business once it has proven demand, with a larger investment and more in-depth evaluation by investors.

7. What do investors look for in Series B funding?

In Series B, investors evaluate:

Revenue Growth: Regular increases in earnings.
Customer Metrics: How many customers are coming in and staying.
Market Position: How well the company competes.
Efficiency: Managing costs while growing.

8. What is post-money valuation?

Post-money valuation is the company's value after a funding round. It equals the pre-money valuation (value before investment) plus the new investment amount. It helps determine how much of the company the new investors own.

9. How do follow-on rounds work?

Follow-on rounds happen when current investors put more money into a company during later funding rounds to maintain or increase their ownership percentage.

10. Why is due diligence important in funding rounds?

Due diligence helps investors verify the company's claims. They review financials, legal compliance, market data, and operations to ensure the startup is a good investment.

11. What challenges do startups face during funding rounds?

Startups often face:

Valuation Disputes: Finding a value both sides agree on.
Standing Out: Attracting investors in a competitive market.
Documentation: Preparing all the necessary details for due diligence.
Dilution: Balancing the need for funds with keeping ownership and control.

Chapter 6: The Role of Venture Capitalists

1. What do venture capitalists do beyond providing funding?

Venture capitalists help startups by:

Mentoring: Guiding founders on strategy and operations.
Networking: Connecting them to customers, partners, and other investors.
Market Insights: Sharing knowledge about trends and competition.
Hiring: Helping find and recruit top talent.

2. How do venture capitalists evaluate founders and teams?

VCs look for:

Experience: Relevant skills and past successes.
Passion: Commitment to the company's vision.
Teamwork: How well the team collaborates.
Problem-Solving: Ability to handle challenges and adapt.

3. Why is due diligence important for venture capitalists?

Due diligence ensures VCs:

Verify the company's claims.
Identify risks and challenges.
Confirm legal and regulatory compliance.
Make informed investment decisions.

4. How do venture capitalists add value to startups?

VCs add value by:

Offering strategic advice.

Helping with financial planning and fundraising.
Joining the board to provide oversight.
Supporting future funding rounds.

5. What do venture capitalists expect from startups?

VCs expect:

Transparency: Regular updates on performance and challenges.
Focus on Growth: Aiming for aggressive growth targets.
Aligned Vision: Shared goals for the company's future.
Exit Plan: A strategy to return their investment, like a sale or IPO.

6. What challenges do venture capitalists face?

Challenges include:

Finding Promising Startups: Identifying real potential in a crowded market.
Managing Investments: Balancing support and oversight.
Market Risks: Handling economic or industry changes.
Exiting Investments: Securing profitable exits, like acquisitions or IPOs.

7. How do venture capitalists assess risks?

VCs assess risks by:

Analyzing the Market: Looking at trends and competition.
Checking Business Models: Ensuring sustainability and scalability.
Reviewing Financials: Evaluating cash flow and spending.
Judging the Team: Trusting the founders to lead effectively.

8. Why are relationships important for venture capitalists?

Relationships help VCs by:

Building trust with founders.
Finding better investment opportunities.
Gaining market insights from industry experts.
Creating connections that benefit their portfolio companies.

9. How can startups communicate well with venture capitalists?

Startups should:

Be Clear: Share updates in a simple and direct way.
Show Progress: Regularly report milestones and results.
Share the Vision: Align with the VC's goals for the company.
Take Feedback: Be open to suggestions and adapt as needed.

Chapter 7: Risks and Rewards of Venture Capital

1. What are the main risks associated with venture capital investing?

The main risks include:

High Failure Rate: Many startups fail, leading to loss of investment.
Market Risk: Changes in markets or consumer preferences can hurt performance.
Operational Risk: Startups might struggle with management or scaling.
Liquidity Risk: It can be hard to sell shares quickly or at a good price.
Dilution Risk: Ownership percentages can shrink in future funding rounds.

2. How do venture capitalists assess risk?

Venture capitalists assess risk by:

Due Diligence: Checking the business model, financials, and team.
Market Analysis: Studying trends, competition, and barriers.
Financial Projections: Reviewing forecasts for potential problems.
Scenario Planning: Considering best, worst, and most likely outcomes.

3. What are the potential rewards of venture capital investments?

The potential rewards include:

High Returns: Successful startups can provide big profits.
Equity Ownership: Shares in startups that may increase in value.
Diversification: Adds variety to investment portfolios.
Supporting Innovation: Backing new ideas can be personally fulfilling.

4. How do successful startups impact venture capital returns?

Successful startups drive returns through:

IPOs: Going public allows VCs to sell shares for high profits.
Acquisitions: Companies buy startups for their technology or market position.
Secondary Markets: Selling shares privately before an IPO or acquisition.

5. Why is diversification important in venture capital investing?

Diversification reduces risk by:

Spreading investments across industries, stages, and regions.
Increasing the chances that a few successful startups will offset losses.

6. What common mistakes do investors make in venture capital?

Common mistakes include:

Skipping Due Diligence: Not checking the startup thoroughly.
Overvaluing Startups: Paying too much based on hype.
Ignoring Trends: Missing market shifts or changes.
Lack of Strategy: Investing without a plan for support and monitoring.

7. How do market conditions affect venture capital investments?

Market conditions can:

Influence Investor Sentiment: Bull markets increase investments; bear markets reduce them.
Impact Exits: Economic downturns limit IPOs or acquisitions.
Affect Valuations: Changing how startups are valued and funded.

8. What strategies can venture capitalists use to mitigate risks?

Strategies include:

Thorough Due Diligence: Checking for red flags before investing.
Portfolio Diversification: Investing in multiple sectors and stages.
Active Management: Helping startups succeed through guidance.

Clear Terms: Protecting interests with well-structured agreements.

9. How can entrepreneurs prepare for the risks of venture capital?

Entrepreneurs can:

Understand Expectations: Be clear about what VCs want in terms of growth and communication.
Build a Strong Business: Create a scalable model with market demand.
Assemble a Great Team: Have skilled and experienced leaders.
Prepare for Due Diligence: Organize financial and operational details.

Chapter 8: Exit Strategies in Venture Capital

1. What are exit strategies in venture capital?

Exit strategies are methods for investors to cash out their investments in a startup, gaining a return on their funding. These strategies are essential for venture capitalists to recover their money and realize profits.

2. Why are exit strategies important?

Exit strategies are important because they:

Define Success: Set goals for how and when returns will be achieved.
Guide Investments: Help VCs decide which startups to back.
Attract Investors: Show potential investors a clear plan for returns.

3. What are the common types of exit strategies?

The common types are:

IPO: Taking the company public and selling shares on the stock market.
Acquisition: Selling the startup to a larger company.
Secondary Sale: Selling shares to another investor before an IPO or acquisition.
Merger: Combining with another company to create a new entity.
Buyback: The startup buys back shares from investors.

4. How does an IPO work as an exit strategy?

Steps in an IPO:

Preparation: Improve finances, governance, and compliance.
Underwriting: Hire banks to manage the IPO and set share prices.
Marketing: Attract investors through roadshows.

Listing: List shares on a stock exchange for public trading.
Selling Shares: Early investors sell their shares to the public.

5. What factors influence the decision to pursue an IPO?

Factors include:

Market Conditions: Favorable markets encourage IPOs.
Growth: Strong performance makes a company ready to go public.
Valuation: A high valuation boosts the attractiveness of an IPO.
Regulation: Costs and requirements affect timing and feasibility.

6. How do acquisitions work as an exit strategy?

Steps in an acquisition:

Find Buyers: Identify companies interested in buying the startup.
Negotiate Terms: Agree on price and deal structure.
Due Diligence: The buyer reviews the startup's finances and operations.
Finalize: Close the deal and distribute returns to investors.

7. What are the advantages and disadvantages of an acquisition?

Advantages:

Quick liquidity for investors.
Access to resources from the acquiring company.
Simplifies the exit process compared to an IPO.

Disadvantages:

Founders may lose control of the company.
Integration into the buyer's operations can be difficult.
Uncertain long-term outcomes for the startup.

8. What is a secondary sale, and how does it work?

A secondary sale happens when early investors sell their shares to new investors. Steps include:

Finding Buyers: Locate investors interested in purchasing shares.
Negotiating: Agree on price and conditions.
Selling Shares: Complete the transaction, providing liquidity to the seller.

9. What should startups consider when planning an exit?

Startups should consider:

Timing: Exit when market and company conditions are optimal.
Valuation: Ensure expectations are realistic.
Alignment: Match exit plans with investors' goals.
Employees: Plan for retention and morale during the exit.

Chapter 9: Current Trends in Venture Capital

1. What are the major current trends in venture capital?

Major current trends include:

Sustainability Focus: Investments in startups addressing environmental and social issues.
Healthtech Growth: Increased funding for telemedicine and health technologies.
Diversity Push: More investment in founders from underrepresented groups.
Remote Work: Rising interest in tools and platforms supporting remote work.
Blockchain and DeFi: Growing investments in decentralized finance and blockchain technologies.

2. How is technology influencing venture capital investments?

Technology is changing venture capital through:

Data Analytics: Using data to evaluate startups and markets.
Online Platforms: Crowdfunding and online investment broaden investor access.
AI and Machine Learning: Streamlining due diligence and identifying promising startups.

3. How are investors approaching sustainability and impact investing?

Investors are:

Prioritizing ESG: Focusing on startups with positive environmental and social impacts.
Measuring Impact: Developing ways to track both financial and social returns.

Creating Thematic Funds: Funding sustainable ventures through specialized investment vehicles.

4. What role do accelerators and incubators play in the current environment?

Accelerators and incubators:

Mentor Startups: Help founders solve early challenges.
Provide Funding Access: Link startups to VCs and angel investors.
Enable Networking: Connect startups with peers, partners, and customers.

5. How is the venture capital environment changing with the rise of diverse founders?

Changes include:

Dedicated Funds: Investments targeted at women, minorities, and other underrepresented founders.
Inclusive Networks: Resources and connections for diverse entrepreneurs.
Diverse VC Teams: Hiring varied talent to reduce investment bias.

6. What are some emerging sectors attracting venture capital attention?

Emerging sectors include:

Healthtech: Telemedicine, personalized care, and health analytics.
Fintech: Digital payments, neobanks, and blockchain.
Edtech: Online learning and educational tools.
Agtech: Sustainable farming and food security innovations.

7. How are valuations being affected in the current venture capital climate?

Valuations are influenced by:

Competition: More investors chasing deals drives valuations higher.
Sector Focus: Interest in trending sectors inflates valuations.
Growth Metrics: Prioritizing revenue growth and user acquisition over profitability.

8. What should entrepreneurs consider when seeking investment in today's market?

Entrepreneurs should:

Align with Trends: Pitch ideas that match investor priorities like sustainability or digital tools.
Prove Resilience: Show how their business can adapt to changes.
Leverage Networks: Use accelerators and industry contacts to connect with investors.

Chapter 10: Building Relationships with Venture Capitalists

1. Why are relationships important in venture capital?

Relationships are important because they:

Build trust between entrepreneurs and investors.
Improve communication and collaboration.
Open doors to mentorship and valuable resources.
Increase chances of success by aligning goals and building long-term partnerships.

2. How can entrepreneurs effectively approach venture capitalists?

Entrepreneurs should:

Research Investors: Understand their focus and portfolio to tailor the pitch.
Craft a Strong Pitch: Clearly present the problem, solution, market, and traction.
Use Warm Introductions: Leverage mutual connections for credibility.
Be Prepared: Anticipate questions and challenges to show readiness.

3. What should entrepreneurs include in their pitch to VCs?

A strong pitch includes:

Problem Statement: What issue does your startup solve?
Solution: How does your product or service address the problem?
Market Opportunity: Data on market size, growth, and competition.
Traction Metrics: Evidence of growth (e.g., users, revenue, partnerships).
Team Strengths: Key skills and achievements of the founders and team.

4. How can entrepreneurs build trust with venture capitalists?

Entrepreneurs can build trust by:

Being Transparent: Share both successes and challenges honestly.
Meeting Milestones: Deliver on promises consistently.
Maintaining Communication: Provide regular updates on progress and changes.
Acting Ethically: Show integrity and sound judgment in decisions.

5. What role does networking play in building relationships with VCs?

Networking helps by:

Facilitating Connections: Meeting potential investors at events and through referrals.
Boosting Visibility: Showcasing your startup to a larger audience.
Building Credibility: Strengthening your reputation with industry leaders and peers.

6. How can startups leverage accelerators and incubators to connect with VCs?

Startups can:

Join Programs: Gain mentorship and exposure to investors.
Attend Demo Days: Pitch to VCs at events hosted by accelerators.
Refine Models: Use the support to improve their business strategy and pitch.

7. What should founders know about investor expectations?

Founders should understand that investors expect:

Clear Communication: Regular updates on progress and challenges.
Realistic Milestones: Achievable goals that reflect growth prospect.
Shared Vision: Alignment on the startup's strategy and direction.
Commitment: A willingness to work collaboratively over the long term.

8. How can founders maintain relationships with VCs post-investment?

Founders should:

Provide Regular Updates: Keep investors informed about performance and plans.
Engage in Decisions: Involve investors in strategic discussions.
Celebrate Success Together: Share wins to cultivate a sense of partnership.
Be Open to Feedback: Actively listen and consider investor suggestions.

9. What common mistakes should entrepreneurs avoid when dealing with VCs?

Avoid:

Overpromising: Making unrealistic claims damages trust.
Being Unprepared: Poor preparation reflects badly on the team.
Ignoring Feedback: Disregarding advice can hinder progress.
Poor Communication: Infrequent updates or unclear messaging erode confidence.

Chapter 11: Resources for Entrepreneurs

1.What types of resources are available for entrepreneurs seeking venture capital?

Entrepreneurs can access:

Books and Articles: Guides and success stories on venture capital.
Websites and Platforms: Databases and tools for finding investors and trends.
Networking Events: Conferences, pitch competitions, and meetups.
Mentorship Programs: Pairing with experienced mentors for advice.

2. What online resources can entrepreneurs use to learn?

Useful online resources include:

Y Combinator's Startup School: Free courses for startups.
Crunchbase: Database of startups and investors.
AngelList: Connects startups with investors and job seekers.
TechCrunch & VentureBeat: Industry news and venture updates.

3. How can entrepreneurs find networking opportunities?

Networking tips:

Attend Industry Events: Go to conferences and pitch events.
Join Organizations: Participate in industry groups and associations.
Explore Meetup and Eventbrite: Look for local workshops and events.
Engage Online: Join LinkedIn groups and other forums.

4. What role do incubators and accelerators play for entrepreneurs?

Incubators and accelerators provide:

Funding: Initial capital for startups.
Mentorship: Guidance from experienced professionals.
Resources: Office space, tools, and support services.
Programs: Structured training and investor connections.

5. What are common mistakes entrepreneurs make when seeking venture capital?

Avoid these mistakes:

Not Preparing: Poorly presented financials or business plans.
Overvaluing: Unrealistic valuations that scare off investors.
Ignoring Investor Focus: Pitches unrelated to VC's interests.
No Follow-Up: Missing chances by neglecting communication.

6. How can entrepreneurs stay informed on venture capital trends?

Entrepreneurs can stay informed by:

Subscribing to Newsletters: Like TechCrunch or CB Insights.
Joining Webinars: Hear insights from industry leaders.
Following Influencers: Track VCs and experts on LinkedIn or Twitter.
Joining Groups: Participate in venture-focused organizations.

7. What online courses can help entrepreneurs learn about venture capital?

Recommended online courses:

Coursera: "Venture Capital and Startup Funding."
edX: "Entrepreneurship in Emerging Economies."
LinkedIn Learning: "Venture Capital: Start to Finish."

8. How can entrepreneurs build a strong support network?

Tips for building a strong support network:

Connect with Peers: Join startup groups and forums.
Find Mentors: Seek guidance from experienced advisors.
Use Alumni Networks: Leverage school or workplace connections.

Attend Events: Meet others through workshops and seminars.

Conclusion

Venture Capital Basics Q&A has explained the basics of venture capital, helping you understand how it works, what it involves, and the key people who play a role in it. Venture capital is about more than just getting money. It's also about building connections, growing your business, and overcoming challenges.

Venture capital helps startups grow by providing funding and support. Understanding the types of investors and their strategies can help you find the right fit for your business. Raising funds involves steps like pitching your idea, showing progress, and negotiating terms. Being prepared is important.

Good relationships with investors bring more than money. They offer advice, guidance, and useful connections. While venture capital has risks, the rewards can be big. Be ready to adjust as you face challenges. There are many tools and resources, like books, online guides, and mentorship, that can help you succeed.

Whether you are a startup founder or an investor, staying informed and open to learning is important. Venture capital is about partnership and turning great ideas into reality. With the knowledge from this book, you are ready to take on challenges, build strong connections, and achieve your goals in entrepreneurship.

www.ingramcontent.com/pod-product-compliance
Lightning Source LLC
Chambersburg PA
CBHW070943220526
45469CB00007B/2502